Bristol Radical Pam

The Cock Road Gang

Steve Mills

ISBN 978-1-911522-29-4

Bristol Radical History Group.
Revised 2021. First Published 2013
www.brh.org.uk ~ brh@brh.org.uk

Introduction

The 'Cock Road Gang' from Kingswood, near Bristol, were perhaps the most notorious criminal gang in Britain in the late 18th and early 19th centuries. This is quite a strong statement, and there is certainly more research to be done. However, the geographical spread of their misdemeanours, the columns of newspapers dedicated to recording their activities and the amount of gang members that were hanged or transported for their crimes demonstrate that they were indeed infamous and very active. It was said that a "gang of desperate villains who were mounted and armed, infested the area."[1] The *Gloucester Journal* went further, stating that the Cock Road Gang were a "gang of desperados" whose activities meant that "no inhabitant felt safe in their own bed" and that "no traveller could pass along the Kingswood Road, without being robbed or molested."[2] This is evidently hyperbole, but residents from this small area were clearly very active in criminal activity. Braine in his work on Kingswood Forest felt that no other village in England surpassed Cock Road for its notoriety in robbery 100 years ago."[3]

It is not clear if the criminals written about within this pamphlet ever considered themselves as an organisation or a 'gang'[4] as the local newspapers screamed in their reports. However, there was evident organisation and co-operation amongst those who lived in the Cock Road area and some families were central to this. Furthermore, the felons lived in a distinct geographical location within the Kingswood area. Cock Road was only a small village, extended from a road. Members of this criminal fraternity also came from neighbouring villages and hamlets. Bitton, Oldland, and Hanham were prominent amongst court reports and newspapers stories as places of residence for those in trouble with the law who were members of the gang. Therefore, the Cock Road Gang was the name given to a group of people by the newspapers and the establishment. There does not appear to be any record of a criminal declaring that they were in, or representing, the so-called 'Cock Road Gang'. However, we have to remember that to have done so would have been suicide, as the judges would have certainly proclaimed the death sentence. Some

---

1 *Felix Farley's Bristol Journal (FFBJ)*, 9 August 1817
2 *Gloucester Journal*, 10 October 1814
3 A. Braine, *A History of Kingswood Forest* (Kingsmead, Bath, 1969) p. 177
4 http://www.wisegeek.com/what-is-a-gang.htm What is a gang? A gang is a group of people which shares an identity and a common purpose. The term has come to be associated specifically with street gangs, which organise for the purpose of carrying out illegal activity. This fits with how the papers, authorities and law-abiding citizens viewed the Cock Road Gang.

families bore the brunt of the authorities' backlash, with brothers, cousins, uncles and fathers all being implicated at particular times. Some wives and mothers, whilst suffering arrest themselves, also lost numerous male relatives to the gallows or transported across to the colonies. Common surnames marble through the records of the gang's activities. The Caines were especially infamous, but also common were Groves, Britton, Wilmot, Ilses, Bryant, Haynes, Brain(e), and Fry.[5]

The history of criminal activity is possibly the most difficult research to undertake. It is fraught with pitfalls, as the accused were hardly likely to admit their actions and the prosecutors also clearly got things wrong from time to time, as they do now. This study does make the assumption, following court reports and newspaper articles, that there was a gang operating in unison, with ties of kinship. It might have been that there were a lot of criminals in this area, and the authorities and the literate class were making the connections. Or perhaps it was in some landowner's interest to increase the hyperbole and fear that there was a criminal gang, completely out of control, terrorising the god-fearing inhabitants of the surrounding area. They would then find it easier to secure convictions, and raise forces to subdue the area, prior to enclosure of the common land. Previous attempts had met with successful community resistance.[6]

The gang's territory was the Kingswood Forest, situated on the outskirts of East Bristol, straddling Gloucestershire, Somerset, and the City and County of Bristol; the forest was a perfect sanctuary, a proverbial 'hole in the wall'. Crimes could be committed in one county, with the perpetrators fleeing to another. Forests had a reputation for being an outlaws' sanctuary; with the semi-fictional Robin Hood being the most renowned, Kingswood was particularly infamous.[7] Many people populating the forest were squatters, using common land sustainably. When Charles Stuart lost his head during the Civil War, there was no overall authority in the forest. After the end of the British Civil War, the unpaid New Model Army was shipped from Bristol to Ireland, in 1649. Some might have decided to stay behind, and the population of Kingswood grew during this period of civil upheaval. Many squatters

5 Bristol Reference Library pamphlet B29688; Ian Wyatt, The Cock Road Gang, PB History V p. 37
6 Steve Mills, *A Barbarous And Ungovernable People–A Short History Of The Miners Of The Kingswood Forest (Bristol Radical History Group: 2009).* Bristol Library: *The Ellacombe Manuscripts*, volume 6, Kingswood, 8, 137, 189, 191, 193, 195, 199, and 205, Volume 7
7 J. Latimer, *Annals of Bristol Volume 3* (Georges, Bristol, 1970 (first printed 1887)) p. 49; R. Malcolmson, "A Set of Ungovernable People: The Kingswood Colliers in the 18th Century", in Brewer and Styles, *An Ungovernable People; The English and their Law in the 17th and 18th Centuries* (Rutgers University Press, 1980) p. 85-127

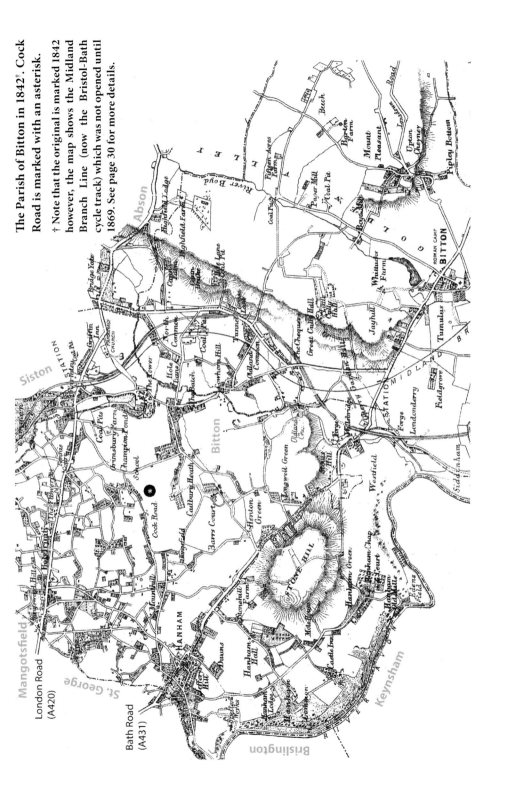

The Parish of Bitton in 1842[†]. Cock Road is marked with an asterisk.

† Note that the original is marked 1842 however, the map shows the Midland Branch Line (now the Bristol-Bath cycle track) which was not opened until 1869. See page 30 for more details.

survived on the commons, in large communities, subsisting on the land and the small coal workings that were scattered throughout the forest. These loose arrangements also strengthened the rights of the larger landowners, some of whom were also squatting.[8] They protected the rights of common, and in turn the numerous smaller holdings would support the larger landowners in a semi-feudal relationship. Subsequent to the restoration of Charles II some of these squatter landlords were granted 'liberties' (see the map on page 14/15), after court proceedings were unsuccessful in regaining the land for the monarchy. *Liberty* is a legal term used to describe disputed land ownership and gave the holder the right or privilege of access to a particular place. Attempts to repossess the land by force, by newly appointed officers of the restored crown, were not successful. In the 1670s Forest Rangers were greeted with large riots and chased away.[9] The parishes of Wick and Abson, Oldland, Hanham, Bitton and Kingswood made the core of the forest and it was these settlements that were home to most of the gang, as recorded in court records and newspapers. Not all felons recorded as gang members came from Cock Road, which was only a small area in the Manor of Gee Moor. It is not completely clear why Cock Road was so infamous, but it would appear that the road overlooked the Bath to Bristol highway, where gang members apparently sat surveying the countryside, waiting for the next mail coach to rob.

Whilst the forest was renowned for sheltering outlaws, it was also essential to the industrial base of Bristol. The trees provided wood for buildings and ships and Gloucestershire weavers provided clothing. But perhaps most important was coal; the forest was dotted with mines. By 1609 many of the trees had gone and coal was already being mined.[10] The job of a miner was a difficult and dangerous one, but it also bred a close community amongst the Kingswood colliers, and they were renowned as a hardy bunch. They were very willing to 'riot' to defend their livelihoods and community. They violently protested against wage cuts, the imposition of tolls on the roads they used to transport their coal and they also used 'collective bargaining by riot' when the price of wheat increased. Many Bristolians, whilst needing their coal, feared and loathed them. The Kingswood colliers were happy to invade Bristol

8 Ian Bishop; *The Cock Road Gang, The story of the Caines Family* (Bishop, Bristol: 2003) p. 2-3; Bristol Library: *The Ellacombe Manuscripts* Volume 6, numbers 8, 69, 137 and 149
9 Ibid. Volume 6, numbers 189, 191, 193, 195, and 205, also Volume 7 Kingswood numbers 14, 17 and 25-7. The latter being the summing up of the court and the Crown's final efforts to 'rescue' the land via the legal system
10 David Rollison; *The local origins of modern society, Gloucestershire 1500- 1800* (Routledge, London, 1992), p. 39

The London mail coach outside the Post Office in Corn Street. John Palmer, a Bath theatre owner, wanted to reduce mail delivery times between cities. He ran the first ever mail coach from the Rummer Tavern in Bristol to Lombard Street in London on 2 August 1784 and instantly reduced the delivery time from 38 to 16 hours (see page 30).

to make demands on the authorities if the need arose.[11] One of their most infamous but also amusing exploits involved bailiffs coming to the forest in an attempt to collect unpaid rents. The bailiffs were met by a group of colliers, who explained the error of their ways before lowering them down a coal pit. The bailiffs were hauled up after a night but would not promise to desist from their efforts to collect the money. Therefore, they were lowered back down with a meal of gin and gingerbread. After a while the bailiffs saw the error of their ways and promised not to return. They were allowed to leave, after paying the colliers three shillings for 'bed and breakfast'.[12] This kind of action had been done before with customs officials during the cider tax disputes in 1763 and it was a marker of their collective strength and willingness to use it.

In the early industrial period, there was a great deal of open class conflict. Changes to the rural scene are relevant here. The relationships of semi-feudalism, with small tenants tied to the land, paying for their holdings by labouring for the landowner, began to change. Agriculture started to industrialise, with landowners using legal and semi-legal means to kick tenants off the land and

11   Steve Mills, *A Barbarous And Ungovernable People–A Short History Of The Miners Of The Kingswood Forest (Bristol Radical History Group: 2009)*, Bristol Radical History Group
12   Bristol Reference Library pamphlet B29688; Ian Wyatt, *The Cock Road Gang*, PB History V p. 37

to renege on 'customary rights'. Typically, Enclosure Acts were employed to remove tenants and deny these rights. These were used throughout the British Isles during the 16th to 19th centuries. As we will see, they were also used as a tool against the gang in 1817. Landowners also utilised machines to reduce the need for labour. These actions forced people off their land and into the factories of the growing cities in industrialising Britain. This is a simplistic synopsis of the rural situation in the late 18th century, but it will suffice for this study. The point needs to be made that these changes were not always accepted by the rural poor. Riots and other forms of civil disobedience were common, and this was certainly the case in Kingswood Forest. Another way the rural poor could fight back was covert criminal activity. Known as 'social crime', these activities often had the backing of the community. Examples include animal maiming, rick burning and stealing of livestock. People would be targeted specifically due to their role in localised class struggle. For example, a local landowner who had just brought a spanking new threshing machine, thereby reducing the need for local labour, could wake up and find their new machine in pieces and some of their sheep missing. The problem for the historian is proving what 'social' crime is, and conversely what is pure 'acquisition' crime. Of course, in serious cases no criminal would willingly give reasons for their crimes unless, of course, they wanted a rope for their neck. However, sometimes careful assumptions, based on evidence, can be made.

Cock Road: The Lie of the Land

The Cock Road Gang certainly targeted people in authority and local landowners. Whilst it can be argued that these people were the only ones with anything worth nicking, other evidence shows that gang members certainly did differentiate. A good example of this behaviour was the collection of protection money. Gang members often collected at Lansdown Fair, just outside Bath, where landowners would be required to pay a type of protection tax, determined by a sliding scale linked to size of estate.[13] The gang also committed acts of arson, animal maiming, and shot out the windows of local grasses and constabulary. It is also worth noting that the gang had wide support in their community and members would be protected. Bristol newspapers regularly stated that the whole community were given to crime and the passing of stolen goods as well as being infamous highway robbers. The main

13 A. Braine, *A History of Kingswood Forest* (Kingsmead, Bath, 1969) p. 91

"Black Giles, the poacher. Containing some account of a family who would rather live by their wits than their work"

"Parley the Porter. An allegory: showing how robbers without can never get into a house unless there are traitors within."

Bath to Bristol highway ran through their heartland. They could gather on one of the hills overlooking the road, picking their victims. The post coach was one of their favourite targets, and these depredations became a major bugbear for the authorities in Bristol, for obvious reasons. Gang members would also turn their hand to horse and livestock stealing with poaching, burgling and pickpocketing in their repertoire. It should be remembered that this was during a time when even minor offences could lead to the ultimate sanction–judicial murder. Those convicted of crimes who escaped the gallows could also face transportation to the colonies, which could mean exile for life.[14]

The Cock Road Gang were quite able to utilise their highway robbery skills beyond the Bath Road. One of the most famous highwaymen in the 18th century came from Cock Road. Richard Haynes (aka Dick Boy) had been a known thief since the age of seven. He became a highwayman, linking up with his friend John Carey. The pair worked the roads surrounding Bristol and enjoyed a reasonably successful career. That is until they tried to rob a Mr Crach near Downend. They fired a pistol at him as he tried to escape and, when they missed, hit him on the head with the butt of the pistol. This killed the unfortunate Mr Crach. The confederates escaped arrest, but only briefly, as they were eventually recognised and apprehended in Taunton. Whilst both were charged, Dick Boy was acquitted but Carey was hanged. His comrade took his body back to Oldland to be buried and then returned to work. Haynes was finally caught in Westminster, London, and transported to

14   J.M.Beattie, *Crime and Courts in England 1660-1800*. (OUP, Oxford, 2002) pp 471-483,500-06.

Highwaymen holding up a coach in 1750.

Botany Bay. Surprisingly, he escaped and eventually returned to Oldland. He did not, however, return alone, bringing with him a young wife, apparently the daughter of a German nobleman. She actually turned out to be from Westerleigh and was eventually hanged in London for a failed robbery. When Dick Boy first returned to England, he did not immediately restart his criminal career, instead he lived quite openly. Haynes was recorded as being big and powerfully built and it comes as no surprise that he became a boxer. Eventually, however, he did return to his old criminal ways, which proved to be his undoing. Haynes was hanged in Bristol on 25th April 1800, after being convicted of shooting at a constable who had tried to arrest him for stealing a silver tankard.[15]

In Braine's *History of Kingswood Forest*, dated 1891, it is recorded that perhaps no other village in England surpassed Cock Road for its notoriety in robbery. It was also recorded as being the home of many 'hucksters' (fences) and that these dealers in stolen goods could be seen passing with their carts but no one dared stop or report them.[16]

John Read and John Ward were convicted of housebreaking in 1781. As he sentenced them to be hanged the judge described them as "part of a desperate gang who terrorised the good people of Bitton and the surrounding area" and that "this gang had long infested the county." They were 'turned off' on 30th

15 Bristol Reference Library pamphlet B29688; Ian Wyatt, *The Cock Road Gang*, PB History V
16 http://www.flickr.com/photos/brizzlebornandbred/3319293364/ "The Kingswood Association, for the prosecution of thieves and housebreakers; prospectus" in Braine, *A history of Kingswood Forest*, pp. 92-3

March 1781.[17] This gives us the first taste of the hype about criminals from the area. It could also be the first use of the word 'gang' to describe the relationship between criminals in this area of the forest. Furthermore, whilst the judge used words like 'infested' to describe the 'gang', he also insinuated that they had been operating for some time.

On the 1st September 1783, some of the Cock Road Gang were caught sheep stealing. James Bryant, Benjamin Webb and George Ward were committed to Tewkesbury gaol. They were charged with killing two lambs which were the property of Isaac Lewis from the parish of Bitton. Webb and Ward had also stolen two horses. Someone clearly had brought them some useful presents, when in Christmas 1783 they managed to saw through their leg irons whilst still in prison. However, the turnkey discovered them before they could make good their escape and had them put in 'widow's arms'. This involved the barbaric punishment of being attached to the prison walls by your arms. Webb and Ward were both eventually hanged in Gloucestershire in March 1784.

Just by coming from the Cock Road area and finding yourself in trouble with the law could prejudice your treatment. For example, Joseph Fry and Samuel Ward were hanged in April 1786, for "minor misdemeanours."[18] They came from the Bitton area, which seemed to increase the need for the ultimate sanction in the judge's eyes.

One of the most interesting features of the Cock Road Gang was the central role of some extended families that were involved. The local press regularly stated that whole families were given to crime alone in order to subsist[19] and evidence from the period seems to correlate with this. One family which often appears in the reports relating to the gang were the Caines.

The Caines Family

The 'Kaynes' family were first recorded in the parish of St Mary's, Bitton, in 1621. Abraham Caines was born in 1707 and was recorded as being a Tythingman of Oldland, in 1722.[20] There was a suggestion that he, his father and siblings were involved in low level crime and Abraham was described as being:

---

17 Ian Bishop, *The Cock Road Gang, The story of the Caines Family* (Bishop Books, Bristol: 2003) p. 11
18 Ibid. p. 13
19 "The Kingswood Association, for the prosecution of thieves and housebreakers; prospectus" in Braine, *A History of Kingswood Forest,* pp. 92-3
20 *FFBJ 30.12.1726.* Ironically, a 'Tythingman' was responsible for law and order within an area, which was one tenth of a hundred, a sub-division of a parish that goes back to Saxon times.

A pickpocket (far left) 'working' a fair, in this case at Vauxhall Gardens in 1805.

one of a gang of notorious robbers & housebreakers. He was taken in parish of Hullavington in particular for stealing 2 sheep from Mr Perker of Bitton & a furnace from Josias Robbings of same. He jumped over a hedge towards a farmer' house where they found him covered with hay.[21]

On 18th March 1726 a sentence of death was passed on Abraham Caines and William Bateman for robberies at Bitton and Mangotsfield. Elizabeth Jones, Caines' mother-in-law was 'burnt in the hand', therefore branded for life for her involvement, though this is not clearly explained or properly recorded. Abraham was eventually executed with Bateman in 1727.[22]

Benjamin Caines, born in 1728, was either a son or cousin to Abraham. Benjamin married Lydia Britton in 1754 and they had four children: Thomas in 1755; Benjamin Junior in 1757; Richard in 1759; and Samuel the eldest in 1754. The only record of Benjamin Senior falling foul of the law was in 1763, when he was convicted of selling beer and fined. He died in 1770, but his name continued and Benjamin Jnr. (now senior) married Ann Cool. They had eleven children together, and seven of their offspring made up the spine of the Cock Road Gang. However, Benjamin Caines did not see all his children grow into adulthood as he was convicted with Joseph Green and William Jeffreys

21 D. P. Lindegaard, *Kingswood Index*, http://www.bristolfamilyhistory.co.uk/kingswood-index
22 Ian Bishop, *The Cock Road Gang, The story of the Caines Family* (Bishop Books, Bristol: 2003) p. 20

of grand larceny in April 1793. He and his fellow prisoners received 7 years transportation for their crimes.

Caines's first born son George was a little luckier than his father at first. George, born in 1777, was renowned with his confederate Frank Britton for 'working' fairs (that is swindling) north of Gloucester and Cheltenham, sometimes even into Wales. This was consistent with the activities of the wider gang where fairs were a prime target for crime. These were large gatherings of farmers, trading produce and livestock, and were also known for partying, with the youth of the period attending in order to drink and 'court'. The fair was a very important social and economic gathering where many of the attendees carried cash on them, and it is no surprise that pickpocketing was rife.

George was eventually nicked in Pontypool after a violent row with a pub landlord. He was searched and counterfeit coins were found on his person and a stolen horse was also accredited to him. George was committed to Monmouth prison in 1799. It was claimed by the prosecution that he was a member of a "gang who frequented country fairs as hawkers and pedlars."[23] He only received a one-year prison sentence though, which was very lenient in relation to passing 'crooked coin' and horse theft. Normally such crimes would equate to transportation at the least, if not capital punishment as in the far less serious case of Fry and Ward noted above.

George's period in prison failed to change his ways. In the summer of 1812 George and Isaac Cox got into a fight with Benjamin Curtis, the Parish of Bitton's constable (which must have been a thankless task). Curtis was in the process of trying to arrest Isaac when George came to the rescue, firing a gun at the constable. George missed Curtis but then proceeded to beat him around the head. The constable bolted for help whilst Caines and Cox made their escape. With George now 'on the run' things began to hot up. James Francis, who was about to give evidence in another case in 1812 concerning the 'gang', had three shots fired through the window of his dwelling. This was a clear but unsuccessful attempt to dissuade Francis from giving evidence and unsurprisingly the Cock Road Gang got the blame. However, by this stage, the 'gang' were not afraid of the local authorities; they would go to extreme lengths to defend themselves and their activities. George was eventually seized, imprisoned, tried and found guilty of attempted murder of a policeman. He was sentenced to hang, but this was commuted to transportation for life. In

23   Ibid p 27

A Portsmouth hulk (probably *HMS York*, see page 30) in 1828.

April 1815, after a period on the 'Portsmouth hulks'[24], he left Britain forever. Interestingly, George survived the ordeal and eventually opened a pub in Australia called the Jolly Sailor, perhaps named after one in Hanham, which it is likely that he frequented.[25]

There were other instances where the gang tried to dissuade persons from giving evidence against them. In 1814, Samuel Palmer, the local constable, had been subpoenaed to Gloucester County Court to give evidence against gang members. His house was surrounded in the middle of the night; his name was called out before his windows were shot out. The mysterious assailants tried to entice him out, but Constable Palmer would have none of it. He escaped with his life and gave evidence the next day.[26] What happened to the plucky Palmer after this incident is not recorded, but it is likely he had to watch his back closely.

Another of the Caines family who fell foul of the law was Francis. In July 1804 he was caught and tried for stealing £400 of fine cloth from a barn

24 The Portsmouth Hulks refer to prison ships that were moored in the harbour at Portsmouth. They were first commissioned after an Act in 1776 and were designed to cope with POWs and later the expanding prison population. Prisoners were normally housed in such prior to transportation. The conditions on board were infamous and as a result many of the inmates died.
25 Ian Bishop, *The Cock Road Gang, The story of the Caines Family* (Bishop Books, Bristol: 2003) pp. 27-31
26 *Bristol Mercury,* 22 August 1814

in Freshford, Somerset. His accomplices were recorded as Thomas Batt and Charles Fuller. Francis is noted in the court records as being an oyster and cider seller. The Freshford 'job' was effectively an early form of ram raid and at first glance it appeared to be a well-cased robbery. The gang smashed their way into a warehouse before taking a large amount of cloth. If they had been successful in their exploits, they would have been rich. However, there were some serious flaws in the plan. Nobody needed the cloth in the local area, it being too fine and with a pattern that was easily identifiable, which made it difficult to fence. Furthermore, they had rented the horse and cart, which was traced to the crime, and then back to them. A hue and cry was raised and the 'ram raiders' were caught and taken to Ilchester. Only Francis was charged, suggesting that the other two may have turned King's evidence and informed on him. This was a fairly common way of avoiding the noose and, in this case, it appears to have worked for Francis's confederates. Francis Caines was hanged in Ilchester in September 1804. He had only just married, and his son Francis was christened where his dad was buried, St Mary's church in Bitton.[27]

One of Benjamin and Ann's daughters, Betty, was also an interesting character, but it was the men in her life who made the headlines. In 1812, when George Caines was involved with the short-lived rescue of Isaac Cox, Betty became implicated after stolen pigs were found in her kitchen. They had tried to arrest her before, but the gang beat back the authorities, who had to regroup, get reinforcements, and come back to effect the arrest.[28]

Betty was married to a Tim Bush who in 1810 appeared in the dock with Tom Wilmot and Joe Willis charged with the capital offence of horse stealing. At Gloucester Assizes, all three tried to claim they were elsewhere, but they were not believed, and the judge sentenced them to death. Luckily for them this was commuted to transportation for life and Betty's husband sailed for the far side of the world in 1813. Betty wasted little time, shacking up with George Groves and, in 1814, had a son, Tom, who eventually used both surnames.[29]

George Groves: Criminal Extraordinaire?

George Groves was central to the Cock Road Gang and was infamous during the period for his criminal exploits. He first came to the attention of the authorities when in 1808, aged 17, he stole a pair of leather breeches, and

27 Ian Bishop, *The Cock Road Gang, The story of the Caines Family* (Bishop Books, Bristol: 2003) pp. 33-7
28 *FFBJ, 5* November1814
29 Ian Bishop, *The Cock Road Gang, The story of the Caines Family* (Bishop Books, Bristol: 2003) pp. 39-40

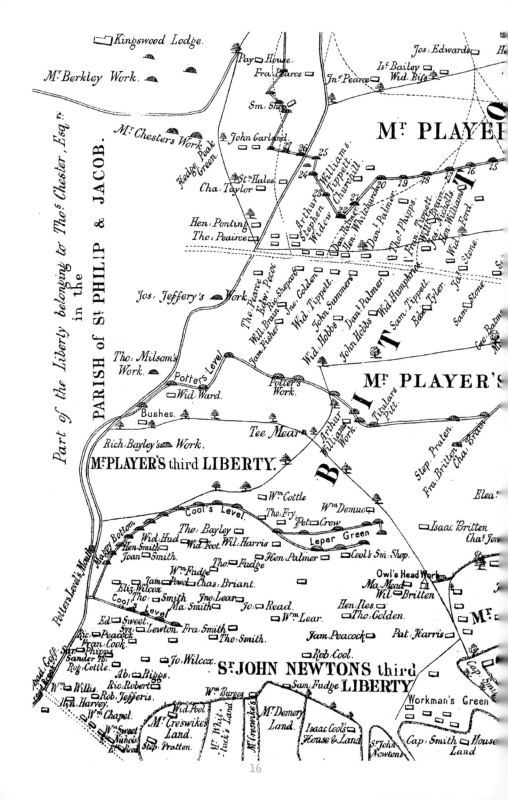

Kingswood Lodge.

Jos: Edwards

Mr Berkley Work.

Pay House.
Fra: Pearce
Is.t Bailey
Jn.o Pearce
Wid: Biss

Sm. Sh.p

Mr PLAYEI

Mr Chesters Work.
John Garland.
27 26 25

Kedge Peak
Kedge Green.
24
Arthur William &
Stephen Tippett
Widow Churchill
20 19 18 17 16 15

St.n Hales
Cha: Taylor
23
22 21
Dan.l Palmer
Hen: Whitchurch
Tho.s Phipps.
Dan.l Palmer
Fran. Tippett.
Will.m Brown.
Hen. Nicholls.
Hen. Williams.
Wid. Ford.

Hen: Ponting
Tho: Pearce
John Stone.

PARISH of St PHILIP & JACOB.
in the
Part of the Liberty belonging to Tho.s Chester, Esq.r

Jos: Jeffery's ⚓ Work.
Tho. Pearce
Edw.d Poole
Rich. Shepard.
Will. Brown.
Jno. Golden.
Wid. Tippett.
John Summers
Dan.l Palmer
Wid. Humphries.
Sam. Tippett.
Barn.d Tyler.
John Stone.
Sam. Stone.
Jam.Fisher.
Wid. Hobbs
John Hobbs
Geo. Palm.

Tho: Milsom's
Work.

Potters Level
Potter's
Work.

Wid. Ward.

Bushes.

Mr PLAYER'S

Rich. Bayley's ⚓ Work.

Tee Mear
Arthur
William's
Work.
Titulars
Pitt.

Mr PLAYER'S third LIBERTY.

B R I T

Step. Praten.
Fra. Britten.
Cha. Brown.

Elea:

W.m Cottle
W.m Demuc
Tho: Fry.
Pet. Crew

Cool's Level.
Leper Green
Isaac Britten
Cha.s Jon

Nappy Bottom
Tho: Bayley
Wid. Hud.
Wid. Foot.
Wil. Harris
Hen. Palmer
Cool's Sm. Shop.

Hen. Smith
Joan Smith
Tho: Fudge
Owl's Head Work
Ma. Mead
Wil. Britten

W.m Fudge
Eliz. Wilcox.
Jam. Powel
Chas. Briant.

Potters Level's Mouth
Cool's Level
Tho: Smith
Jno. Lear
Ma. Smith
Jo. Read.
W.m Lear.
Hen. Iles.
Tho. Golden.

Mr

Ed. Sweet.
Sys. Lewton.
Fra. Smith
Tho. Smith.
Jam. Peacock
Pat. Harris

Ric. Peacock
Fran. Cook.
Str. Phipps.
Sander Po.
Rob. Cottle.
Jo. Wilcox.
Rob. Cool.

Ab: Biggs.
St. JOHN NEWTONS third
Cap. Smi

W.m Willis.
Ric. Robert.
Rob. Jefferis.
Jen. Harvey.
W.m Burges
Sam. Fudge
LIBERTY
Workman's Green

W.m Chapel.
Wid. Pool.
Mr Demery
Land.
Isaac Cool's
House & Land.
Cap. Smith
House
Land

W.m Sweet
Mr Cres-
-wike's
Land.
Mr Whit-
-luck's Land.
Mr Creswike's
St. John
Newtons

Step. Protten.

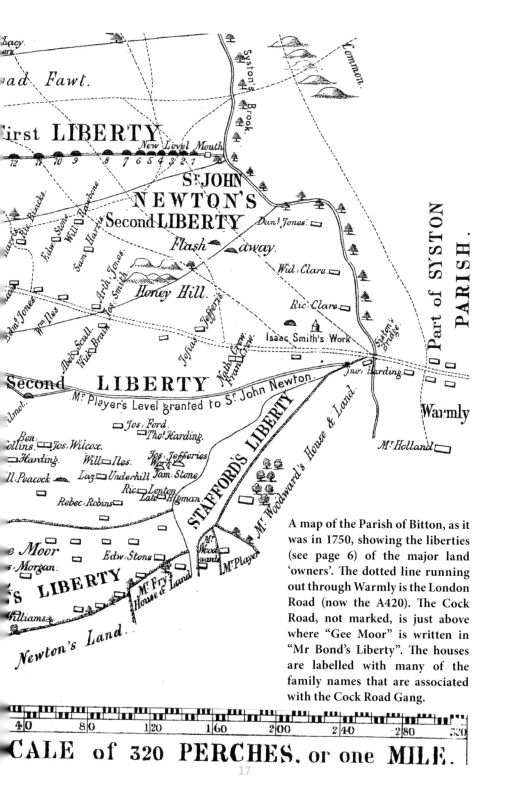

A map of the Parish of Bitton, as it was in 1750, showing the liberties (see page 6) of the major land 'owners'. The dotted line running out through Warmly is the London Road (now the A420). The Cock Road, not marked, is just above where "Gee Moor" is written in "Mr Bond's Liberty". The houses are labelled with many of the family names that are associated with the Cock Road Gang.

subsequently other stolen items were found at his parents' house in Bitton. As a result, he received six months hard labour, to be served at Lawfords Gate House of Correction.[30] Hard labour did not change his habits and he continued a life of crime. In 1809, whilst supposedly hawking gingerbread at Chepstow wool fair in June, he was arrested for pickpocketing. Groves was incarcerated again for six months.[31] A year later he was charged with highway robbery and tried at Bristol Assizes. Groves turned King's evidence leading to the conviction of his two accomplices. At the following Assizes, he was back in front of the beak again, this time charged with burglary. Groves had a strong alibi, confirmed by several others; however, once again he offered evidence against two others tried with him. Both were transported for life.[32] Rather surprisingly his grassing did not put off the ladies; he married Betty shortly after, in 1814.

In February 1817 the Groves' marital bliss was interrupted by another brush with the law; once again, a serious capital charge. Under the oath of Samuel Snell, George was charged with receiving a large quantity of 'bombazet', a type of thin woollen cloth that may be either plain or twilled. The case received extensive attention in the *Felix Farley's Bristol Journal,* a popular local paper from the time. The editor celebrated the fact that Groves had finally been captured after being at large for a long period. It was also noted that he had been clapped in irons after an escape attempt had been foiled.[33] The main witness against Groves and the gang that actually stole the cloth was a girlfriend of one of the burglars. She claimed that four men had combined in the theft, and that they all knew Groves.[34] She added that George was well known to be "the common receiver of goods stolen by any of the gang in Bristol." Three of the burglars refused to speak, but one, Richardson, admitted theft and stated that they had sold the cloth to Groves. Furthermore, the cloth had been discovered after searching one of Groves' houses. He was further implicated by the testimony of a tailor who claimed that he had fashioned a number of articles at Groves' behest from the distinctively patterned cloth. It appeared that George was done for.

---

30 Lawfords Gate was situated on the outskirts of Bristol. The gate stood where Trinity Road Community Centre and police station now stand. The main road to Bath would feed into the city of Bristol via this gate.
31 Bristol Reference Library pamphlet B29688; Ian Wyatt, *The Cock Road Gang*, PB History V pp 1-6
32 Bristol Record Office BRO/JQS/P/270 and BRO/JQS/D/1
33 *FFBJ*, 8 and 15 February, 8 March 1817
34 The other three were William Williams, John Perks, and Richardson; Bristol Record Office BRO/JQS/p/270/ bundle

As Groves waited in the cells in shackles, the situation dramatically changed, when two inmates, including Richardson, escaped from Bristol Newgate prison. Rewards of five and ten guineas were offered for their capture, the higher amount for the witness against Groves. With the chief witness absconded, the case against Groves collapsed and his charmed life continued. Richardson's two accomplices were not so lucky; each was transported for seven years.[35] Groves continued to avoid prison and transportation. He was arrested and freed again in 1819, but his most daring escape occurred in 1820. Groves had been arrested for his old trade of pickpocketing and it was felt prudent to transfer him to the authorities in Bristol, avoiding populated areas whilst doing so. Three men, probably officers of the court, accompanied their prisoner along the Weston Court Way near Kingswood, skirting nearby villages on route. The group were approached by a "gang of well-dressed men" and after a brief exchange of words they departed with the liberated George Groves.[36]

Groves was extremely fortuitous, though his luck may have had something to do with his numerous contacts and benefactors. During times of need he had informed on associates and yet still enjoyed protection. Tracing his career through court reports, newspapers and poor law records, it transpires that he owned numerous properties around Bristol, including in well-to-do St Paul's. He was directly involved in or instigated a myriad of crimes ranging from pickpocketing and burglary to highway robbery and he was a major 'fence' in the city. Groves' charmed existence suggests that he held an important role in the 'gang', more than just a connection by marriage to Betty. It appears that Groves was an important link with the underworld of Bristol and the records show that it proved nearly impossible for the authorities in the city or Gloucestershire to secure a conviction. It is no surprise that Groves was eventually taken, tried and transported, after being arrested in Derby.[37]

35 Bristol Record Office BRO/JQS/D/5; BRO/JQS/P/356; *FFBJ*, 5 March 1817
36 *FFBJ*, 11 September 1819 and 1 July 1820
37 Ian Bishop, *The Cock Road Gang, The story of the Caines Family* (Bishop Books, Bristol: 2003) p. 42

Reaction and Resistance

Back in Cock Road, events had taken a turn for the worse. At the Assizes where Groves was acquitted for the receiving of the bombazet, Vicary Gibbs, the judge presiding, noted the large number of prisoners before him.[38] By 1817 the Napoleonic War was over, with negative effects on the local economy. Large scale military demobilisation and a shrinking workforce led to a significant rise in crime.[39] This worried the bourgeoisie, as they needed to protect their standing and property. Consequently, the lawless residents of Cock Road would have to be dealt with. A local yeomanry was raised, calling itself the Bitton Cavalry. They were quickly called into service and set about clearing the area of criminals.

In June 1817, the local constabulary attempted to execute a warrant on an unrecorded set of lodgings. Some men were arrested and taken to the local lock-up in Bitton. The gaol was then assaulted by a large group of men, shots were fired and dynamite was utilised to effect a release. The next day the constabulary returned, accompanied by the Bitton cavalry, better armed and ready for the worst. They surrounded the Bitton area, recaptured the escaped prisoners and also arrested the ring leaders of the 'riot' and breakout, but took no further chances by taking the prisoners directly to Gloucester Gaol. Attempts were stepped up by the authorities to 'civilise' the area and money was raised to improve the local school. The Bitton Cavalry remained in the area to 'pacify' the population and were successful in arresting the so called 'captain' of the Cock Road Gang, Thomas Caines. He was found in the possession of bags of wheat by a private of the Bitton Cavalry. Caines was charged with aiding and abetting the theft and taken to Gloucester prison with his neighbours and family.[40]

The gang hit back. A dwelling house of a Mr Mountain situated just outside Cock Road in Whitehall, Bristol, was entered by three men in disguise. They took a box containing £6, belonging to a private club. This money had been raised to fund the cavalry and the local school. It would appear that the Cock Roadians had different ideas on how best to utilise these funds. The private club made a plea for further funds and stated that residents of Cock Road were not "responding to philanthropists…they have no morality or virtue". They stated that they needed more money to bring them to justice.[41]

38 FFBJ, 19 April 1817
39 Steve Mills, "Juvenile Crime in Bristol" in Peter Wardley (ed.), *Bristol Historical Resource CD*, (UWE, 2000)
40 *FFBJ*, 21 and 28 June, 5 and 12 July 1817
41 *FFBJ*, 9 August 1817

"The grand assizes: or general gaol delivery."

"The execution of Wild Robert. Being a warning to all parents."

Early in 1871, Benjamin Caines Jnr. was arrested with three others and charged with burglary. He was accused of breaking and entering Sarah Prigg's house armed with a pistol and a sword. He treated the elderly lady and her nephew, who happened to be staying there, roughly. Ben Caines was well known to the establishment. He had only just been acquitted of attacking two constables during the Lent Assizes in Gloucestershire.[42] Ben Caines was taken on the nephew's testimony as he had recognised one of the men who had let his mask slip. This arrest led to reprisals against the local constable. It was reported that a "gang of desperate villains" who were mounted and armed, burnt the corn ricks and barns of a Mr Abbot. They then houghed (cut the tendons) and maimed the constable's horse. He was woken by his dog, and on looking out his window spied a gang of men outside. He opened fire, which they immediately returned. Eventually the 'gang' fled, but not before also houghing the constable's cow.[43]

At the next Gloucestershire Assizes, Thomas Caines was sentenced to seven year's transportation and his brother Benjamin to be hanged. The judge said of Benjamin that he should be hanged in chains after his execution as an example to the other gang members. However, the judge was quickly dissuaded, and no such example was attempted. Needless to say, the sentences did little to pacify Cock Road and more animal maiming occurred. The authorities were

42 Gloucestershire Record Office; GRO/Q/GC5/1
43 *FFBJ*, 9 and 16 August 1817. Houghing involves cutting the animal's hamstring, or tendons, thereby maiming it. This may seem extremely barbaric to the 21st century reader. However, people from 19th century had a completely different relationship to animals than we do today. Houghing is more akin in the current age to torching someone's Porsche or sabotaging plant machinery.

rattled to such an extent the Prince Regent offered a free pardon to anyone giving information that would lead to a conviction. The Cock Road Gang were directly mentioned in his address to the literate of Bristol via the *Felix Farley's Bristol Journal*.[44] The free pardon, however, did not extend to the perpetrators of the crimes. Nor did it seem to have a lot of effect on the gang, as the fire fights continued.

On 6th September 1817, Benjamin Caines took to the scaffold with bravery and was 'turned off' in front of a large crowd. Rather than being hanged in chains, his family recovered the cadaver and returned it to Bitton. Benjamin Senior displayed the body in his pantry, charging a fee for a viewing. The subscriptions raised helped pay for the funeral. On the two-mile walk to the burial ground, a large procession accompanied the coffin, which was attended by six young women dressed completely in white. Benjamin was buried in the same grave as his brother Francis who had been hanged in 1804. The vicar giving the service was reported as saying, "let he that stole, steal no more", as they lowered the body into the grave.[45]

After the execution of Benjamin Caines, the gang went on a rampage. They directed their ire at the authorities and their servants. Constable George Haskins had his horse killed, livestock were maimed, and more ricks and barns burnt. Gun battles broke out several times. Calm was eventually restored and the prominence of the Caines family declined. But over a four-year period, from 1817 to 1821, 16 men and one woman were transported from Cock Road as the authorities tidied up the remnants of the gang.[46]

It was not until 1825 that a Caines once again faced a capital charge. The Tennis Court Inn murder involved an argument between neighbours regarding wandering animals. Roving animals were a common sight in 18th century England, and the animals could be impounded. This is what started the argument. The quarrel continued down the pub, a fight ensued, and a man was killed. Several men were tried, but only two were convicted, on very dubious evidence. One of these was a James Caines.[47] However, this is hardly evidence of a surviving criminal gang.

44 *FFBJ*, 6 September 1817
45 *FFBJ*, 13 September 1817; Ian Bishop, *The Cock Road Gang, The story of the Caines Family* (Bishop Books, Bristol, 2003) pp. 64-70
46 Bristol Reference Library pamphlet B29688; Ian Wyatt, *The Cock Road Gang*, PB History V; P Lindegaard, "The Mark of Cain; The Cock Road Gang", in *Avon Past* no. 8 Spring 1983
47 Ian Bishop, *The Cock Road Gang, The story of the Caines Family* (Bishop Books, Bristol: 2003) pp. 78-92. Similar surnames crop up again, Wilmot, England, Britton, and Peacock. The evidence was a broken knife, but more bizarrely an imprint of a trouser in a muddy verge.

Pacification of Cock Road

As stated previously, the post-Napoleonic war economic downturn corresponded with a large increase in crime in Bristol and across the country.[48] Wheat harvests were poor, and magistrates stepped up efforts against adulterated and under-weight loaves of bread at market, introduced soup kitchens, and ensured that the populace was fed.[49] This was a clear indication that they wanted to pacify a hungry populace and avoid civil disobedience or 'riot'. The newspapers were full of stories of gangs roaming the streets of Bristol. Indignant journalists were calling for all sorts of measures such as young, fit and properly paid night watchmen or even the creation of a 'police force' (what a barmy idea). Subscriptions were being raised for a new prison,[50] as the bourgeoisie of Bristol were becoming increasingly concerned about being overrun by criminals. Convictions rose for several reasons, mainly due to the end of the Napoleonic wars and the demobilisation that followed which had a distinct effect on Bristol's economy. Bristol was famous for her brass cannons, and ship building and many of the weavers in Gloucestershire were employed in making sail cloth or soldiers' uniforms. These jobs became redundant as war needs declined. Furthermore, the large-scale demobilisation exacerbated the effect on the unemployment levels, as most of the returning men were young and fit. Rather than starve, some people had to resort to whatever they could to feed their families, thereby leading to an increase in crime and, as a result, near panic gripped the bourgeoisie.

The Kingswood Association, first formed in December 1811, was a direct response to the level of crime in the area and was modelled on similar associations of the bourgeoisie in other areas which would form, arm and patrol, and also support each other financially to pay for the costs of prosecution. The organisation in Kingswood was no different. In their opening arrangement statement, they

48 *FFBJ* 21 April 1810, 17 July 1813, *Great Increase in Somerset*, 12 April 1817, 19 April 1817. Vicary Gibbs actually made a statement at the beginning of Assizes. 3 May 1817, 11 April 1818, this notes an increase in crime across the country. The increase in crime due to the demobilisation after the war is covered in D.Hay, "War, Dearth, and Theft in the 18th Century; The records of the English Courts", in *Past and Present* no. 95 1982, pp 115-39. See also C. Emsley, *Crime and Society in England 1750-1900* (Longman, London, 1997) p. 25. Bristol had other distinct problems as we have already seen in the discussion about the war economy. Also of interest is the press gang. They were very active in the city during the Napoleonic war. Having cleared the streets, imprisoned felons would be given the choice. Face the slow justice system in a disease-ridden overcrowded cell or join the army or navy. At least you would get a gun I suppose. But after the war the press gangs were ruled out.

49 *FFBJ*, 28 July 1810 discusses an Oxford baker having loaves seized, but as a warning to Bristol, 25 February 1815, 7 and 14 October 1815, 16 March 1816, 23 November 1816

50 *FFBJ*, 20 September 1817. Curiously, one of the main drivers was a Mr Mills. Nothing to do with me or my family, I can assure you.

were clear that they were associating due to the increase in crime and the perceived impotency of the authorities. As far as the 'association' was concerned criminals were not only diverting 'honest' workmen from trade but also educating youth in their ways. The Kingswood Association wanted to "strike a decisive blow to the root of their [the criminals'] system". It was therefore "urgent that they secured convictions quickly."[51] Stephen Cave chaired a meeting, in 1816, with similar intent. The gathering was devoted to the suppression of the Cock Road Gang. The Kingswood Association, the Bitton Cavalry and the authorities in Bristol all joined forces. In the end the Cock Road area was surrounded, and every male marched off to a lock-up in Bristol. Guns, nets and snares were seized, and dogs executed.[52]

For the Kingswood Association blatant power "would not be enough and, to back this up, civilising" efforts were required; a good Christian education was perceived to fulfil this role. Also, land ownership would have to be re-negotiated and the commons, which fed and housed the poor, would have to be enclosed. As with the Kingswood colliers before them, the Wesleyan Methodists' religion and education were aimed at the 'pacification' of rebellious populations.[53]

The building of a new school was intended to attack the source of the 'criminal' culture of Cock Road. In its wake were churches and religious instruction. Newspapers of the period speak about the 'civilising' and pacifying effects of education could have on the young. *Felix Farley's Bristol Journal* even went as far as to lay guilt at the door of the Bristol bourgeoisie. They suggested it was a duty to pay subscriptions to the school and civilise the locals.[54] It was felt that this was a key measure to deflect the youth, early in their lives, from a life of crime. This was well before the Foster Education Act (1870) brought in mass education and gave local authorities the right to raise funds and build schools. In the early 19th century, it was only the well-to-do in Bristol who

51 A. Braine, *A History of Kingswood Forest* (Kingsmead, Bath, 1969) pp. 92-3. There is a full account and their original statement of articles, with subscribers.
52 A. Braine, *A History of Kingswood Forest* (Kingsmead, Bath, 1969) p. 94. However, Braine states this happened in 1815, and 25 men from the area were in Gloucester Jail awaiting trial. This is true, but most were acquitted. I believe that it happened twice, not once as he suggests. This was after the unsuccessful attempt to secure Betty, see above page 7. It also happened after the arrest of Benjamin in 1817. This was far more successful, and 22 men were tried at Gloucester Assizes that year, including Thomas Caines for stealing wheat *FFBJ*, 21 June and 5 July 1817. See page 9. However, also of note is that the offer of a Royal pardon and further attacks on the local constable were still occurring in September.
53 Steve Mills, *A Barbarous and Ungovernable People–A Short History of the Miners of The Kingswood Forest*, (Bristol Radical History Group: 2009)
54 *FFBJ*, 16 November 1816. It should also be noted that this was understood in the same way as missionaries going to foreign shores. Doctors were also going to be on hand, giving smallpox inoculations for free. This would have been popular.

could afford education for their children. However, during the period of this study, money was raised for a school at Cock Road. The gang may have seen that the use of education could and was being used to undermine their way of life. As the Kingswood Association wrote in their articles, it was felt that children were being trained in crime. The Bristol Methodist Sunday School Society, with support from the Kingswood Association, set to work and built the school which was situated right in the middle of Cock Road. It was well attended, and the boys were said to get up by 4am.[55] Time-work discipline indeed. Religion was also employed, with subscriptions and church attendance imposed. Later in the period, youth were prosecuted for not attending church and playing games on a Sunday.[56] However, in 1817, the school was burgled by criminals, who made away with mathematical instruments and books.[57]

The enclosing of common land consolidated these efforts of control, as squatters lost their customary rights and land. However, it is important to note that the large squatters who had secured 'liberties'[58] were left unmolested. The enclosure of common land was advertised in *Felix Farley's Bristol Journal* in 1819.[59] In August 1819 the last remnants of the gang were rounded up. Lydia Caines had her house searched and a Robert England was arrested. It was said that he was a "notorious thief" from the area. He was charged with and eventually convicted of stealing wheat from Mr Shaw, the proprietor of the George Inn. In the same month, in the Old George Inn[60], a meeting took place to discuss the encroachments on the recently enclosed lands in Bitton. At the same public house, 40 lots of land were sold in Oldland, Longwell Green, North and Hanham Commons, all within the area within this study.[61] These sales continued, and more lots were sold at the Old George Inn in 1821. Those that would lose their homes were also listed; the Brittons, Bryants, Stone, Peacock and Frys, not forgetting widow Isles.[62] There were no Caines family members

55 A. Braine, *A History of Kingswood Forest* (Kingsmead, Bath, 1969) pp. 94-95; E.P Thompson, *Customs in Common* (Penguin, London, 1991) pp. 380-92 and 394
56 Bristol Library: *Ellacombe Manuscripts*, Volume 7, Kingswood no. 150; This is a handbill 28 February 1824, giving a caution to Sabbath breakers. It continued stating that anyone found playing, gambling or having any time that could be seen as fun, would be locked up. Document no. 151 names two young men, Ben Skull and John Stone who had been caught having fun and had been punished. Both gave assurances of future good behaviour. Also, in this bundle of manuscripts and documents are letters to the Lord Sidmouth, the Home Secretary after the Napoleonic war pleading for support in the suppression of the gang; Document no. 139.
57 *FFBJ*, 15 November 1817
58 See page 6
59 *FFBJ*, 26 June 1819
60 The author is not sure if this is the exact same public house.
61 *FFBJ*, 21 and 28 August, 18 September 1819
62 Bristol Library: *Ellacombe Manuscripts*, Volume 9, Bitton Oldland, document nos. 89 and 96

mentioned, they had all 'gone' in one way or another. Benjamin (see family tree) Caines had had eleven children, including seven sons. As a result of the Cock Road conflict two had been hanged and three transported, one had died. Elizabeth Caines (aka Betty) had lived with three men, two of whom were transported. Similarly, Lydia Caines had lived with three men, all of whom ended up in the Antipodes.

Conclusion

What evidence is there that there was a social enterprise like a 'gang' operating in the Cock Road area? As we have seen, the actual definition of a 'Cock Roadian' was loose. To be considered a member one would hail from what was then known as Kingswood Forest, which encompassed several parishes. It is probable that some that newspapers declared people as being 'gang members' who were nothing of the sort.[63] They may have come from the area and were caught committing crime, but this did not mean they were part of the so-called Cock Road Gang. Whilst some links are clear, with 'family' being the easiest marker for the historian to recognise, nobody charged every declared their membership of the Cock Road Gang. However, of course, to do so would have been literally suicidal.

There is no doubt that there was an element of hysteria amongst property holders. They were generally worried about crime. *Felix Farley's Bristol Journal* was full of stories of robberies and 'gangs' operating in and around Bristol. There were regular proposals for a new gaol and police force in the press, therefore it is unsurprising that editors might exaggerate and bias their reporting of events, such as highlighting a supposed 'conspiracy' between criminals. The authorities got their new jail in 1816, though it was later burnt down during the 1831 'riots'.[64] Also the first government acts designed to create a national police force, were being proposed and debated, leading eventually to the Metropolitan Police Force Act of 1829. The fear of the 'criminal' and the supposed 'breakdown of society' was a national talking point.

Was the existence of a 'gang' on the outskirts of Bristol over-egged to support these changes in the law? There was certainly some organisation

63 Defining a 'gang', 'gang members' and 'gang affiliates' is apparently a perennial problem for the authorities. In 2011 after the August 'riots' in the U.K., the principal report by the Home Affairs Committee stated categorically: "The Home Secretary should clarify what the Home Office means by the term ['gang'] in the context of the August disorder and the methodology used to establish whether a particular individual was 'affiliated to a gang'" *Policing Large Scale Disorder*, August 2011.
64 For more details of the New Gaol see http://mshed.org/explore-contribute/themes/transforming/transforming-places-of-power-and-influence-control/bristol-new-gaol/

The gate house of the New Gaol By Samuel Loxton c1900. Commissioned in 1816 to replace Bristol's aging prisons (including Newgate Gaol) the New Gaol was opened in 1820, only to be burnt down in the 1831 riots. It was repaired and finally closed in 1883 when it was replaced by Horfield Prison. The prison was demolished in 1895, apart from the gatehouse which can still be seen on Cumberland Road.

and confederation between criminals in the Kingswood area. Major crimes often need planning and division of labour, so it is no surprise that some organisation and communication between criminals was present. There were certainly some links, based around family and locality, though it was not easy for the authorities (or the 21st century historian) to ascertain these. The area of Kingswood was seen as a different community. The miners were perceived to be a rebellious lot, given to rioting and having common customs and practices rather than respect for the law. There were distinct differences in everyday life due to the nature of forest work, usage of common land and in the hard and dangerous work the colliers engaged in. As we have seen, there is evidence of organisation along family lines. However, there is no record of initiation rites or the young actually being schooled in criminal activities. The latter was widely suggested in the press though, but was this just part of the hyperbole? The lack of evidence is not surprising as the criminal is not likely to provide confirmation of this—a typical problem when analysing 'social crime'. Perhaps the strongest indication is the solidarity exhibited when rescuing felons from the authorities. On several occasions, rescues were effected by criminals grouping together to attack lock-ups, prisoners en-route and gaols. The whole village and surrounding hamlets would rise in defence of the 'felons' and this appears to have happened on numerous occasions. This would have been part of an oral tradition, as the Kingswood squatters of 1670 sent the Kings-men packing.[65] The Colliers were famous for ripping down toll booths, and invading Bristol when the price of bread increased. So it is perhaps unsurprising that the people of Cock Road rose when, for example, the establishment tried to take Betty and her pigs. This suggests that *confederacy and conspiracy* were employed to deal with a situation which motivated many to act.

The Cock Road families which sustained and nurtured the 'gang' intermarried and lived in close proximity. To defeat them the authorities had to surround the area and make mass arrests. After the 'ring leaders' were taken, more subtle methods were utilised. Residents of the area were forced into church and were supervised by the parish officials who doled out poor relief. The young were disciplined and schooled in basic Maths and English, but also in religion and their place in society. In the Ellacombe manuscripts it is written that:

this gang has been broken up by the establishment of schools. Cock Road, once a city of refuge for army deserters and outlaws of every kind is now quiet, peaceable and orderly as any place perhaps in the county of Gloucestershire

The manuscript continues suggesting that merit for this 'success' should go to the Methodists.[66] However, there were other powerful forces behind these relatively benign pacifiers. The Kingswood Association was set up to monitor and help suppress criminal activity and had the support of the armed force of the establishment. Finally, common land was enclosed. This undermined customary rights and took subsistence from the squatters and colliers, making it harder for them to make ends meet, and thus they became semi-reliant on the 'controlled' poor relief. Here is a textbook response to an independent community that had oppositional values and lifestyles, from a concerned bourgeoisie determined to retain control over and safeguard their property. The mines no longer exist, there is now a large shopping mall on the High Street; but there are still Caines listed in the phone book. They survived it all.

65 Bristol Library: *The Ellacombe Manuscripts*, volume 6, Kingswood, 8, 137, 189, 191, 193, 195, 199, and 205
66 Bristol Library: *Ellacombe Manuscripts*, Volume 7 Kingswood, 157

Acknowledgements

Firstly, I would like to thank all of BRHG for inspiration and support. All these years, and we still have the same ethos and direction. These comrades are a joy to work with. I would like to thank Will for his patient proff readiong, and Roger for the suggested corrections, which I then changed much to his amazement; his patience is also legend. A special thanks to Dawn who whilst fighting tirelessly to keep libraries public, still found time to search for supporting pictures. Lastly, much respect to me Boys, William and Pierre, who are my main inspiration.

Steve Mills, October 2013

Picture Credits

BRHG would like to thank Dawn Dyer for finding the pictures from Bristol Central Reference Library. For permission to reproduce them please email refandinfo@bristol.gov.uk.

Front Cover: Detail from "The Liberty of the Subject" by James Gillray, 1779.

Page 5: "Map of the Parish of Bitton, Gloucestershire. From the Ordinance Map By Cotterells and Cooper, 1842" Plate I from *The History of the Parish of Bitton, in the County of Gloucester* by Rev. H. T. Ellacombe (William Pollard, Bristol: 1881)‡. Found in Bristol Central Reference Library. For more details about the date of the Midland Branch Line see www.avonvalleyrailway.org/historical/midland-railway.

Page 7: "The Post Office Bristol, Arrival of the London Mail" by (Isaac) Robert Cruikshank, 1826. For more on the history of the mail coach see postalheritage.org.uk/page/Mail-Coaches.

Page 9: "Black Giles, the poacher. Containing some account of a family who would rather live by their wits than their work" and "Parley the Porter. An allegory: showing how robbers without can never get into a house unless there are traitors within" from the *Cheap Repository Tracks*.† Found in Bristol Central Reference Library.

Page 10: "An Exact Representation of Maclaine the Highwayman Robbing Lord Eglington [sic] on Hounslow Heath on the 26th June. 1750" by Charles Mosley. © Trustees British Museum.

Page 12: Detail from "One half of the world don't know how t'other lives. Sung by Mr Dignum at Vauxhall Gardens" 1805. © Trustees British Museum.

Page 14: "Prison-Ship, in Portsmouth Harbour" from *Fifty Plates of Shipping and Craft Drawn and Etched by E.W. Cooke*, 1829. © Trustees British Museum. For a biography of *HMS York* see www.portcities.org.uk/london/server/show/conMediaFile.1206/Prison-ship-York-at-Portsmouth-Harbour.html

Page 16-17: Detail from "A Plan of Mr Player's Manors and that of Sr John Newton's &c., lying in the Parishes of Bitton and Mangotsfield truly transcribed from Mr Player's original Plan Dated 1750 By Daniel Cook, 1779." Plate XI from *The History of the Parish of Bitton, in the County of Gloucester* by Rev. H. T. Ellacombe (William Pollard, Bristol: 1881)‡. Found in Bristol Central Reference Library.

Page 21: "The grand assizes: or general gaol delivery" and "The execution of Wild Robert. Being a warning to all parents" from the *Cheap Repository Tracks*.† Found in Bristol Central Reference Library.

Page 27: Entrance to the Old Gaol New Cut Partly Demolished by Samuel Loxton c1900. Found in Bristol Central Reference Library.

Back Cover: Adapted from the "The trial and execution of Richard Gillam for the murder of Mary Bagnall at Bath", *Bath Single Sheets*, 1827. Found in Bristol Central Reference Library.

†The *Cheap Repository Tracks* were a series of moralistic stories conceived and largely written by Hannah More to encourage worthy reading in the newly educated 'lower' classes. They were originally published 1795-98 but appeared in various permutations well into the 19th century. To find out more see http://digital.library.mcgill.ca/chapbooks/index.php. Full free copies can downloaded from Google Books.

‡A free copy can be downloaded from archive.org and openlibrary.org.

The Caines Family Tree

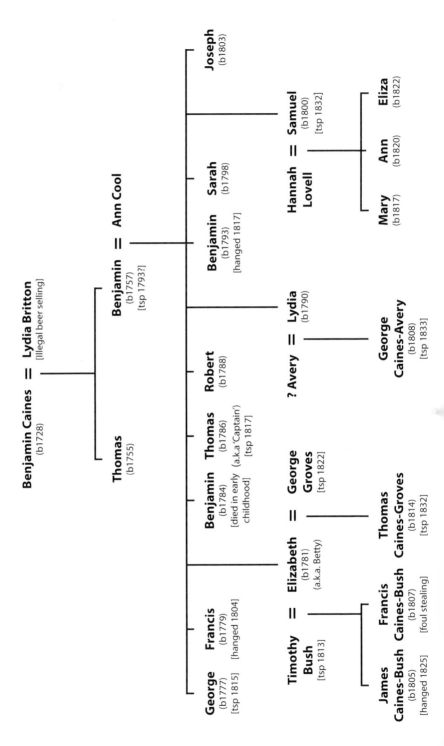